BREAKING THE STIGMA

MEN'S MENTAL HEALTH IN THE MODERN WORLD

REMI KUTI

Table of Contents

Introduction

Definition of men's mental health

Defining men's mental health is a critical step in breaking the stigma surrounding mental health issues in men. Men's mental health refers to the overall wellbeing of men's emotional, psychological, and social functioning. It encompasses a broad range of mental health conditions, including depression, anxiety, PTSD, trauma, anger management, emotional regulation, addiction, substance abuse, relationship and marriage counseling, stress and burnout prevention, suicide prevention, crisis intervention, body image, self- esteem, career and workplace mental health, spirituality, and mindfulness practices.

Depression and anxiety are prevalent in men and can significantly impact their mental health. Men's PTSD and trauma are also common, often resulting from military service, accidents, or abuse. Men's anger management and emotional regulation are essential for managing stressors and improving relationships. Men's addiction and substance abuse can lead to severe consequences, including physical and mental health problems, financial difficulties, and legal issues.

Relationship and marriage counseling is critical for men who struggle with interpersonal issues. Men's stress and burnout prevention are essential for maintaining work-life balance and avoiding chronic stress. Men's suicide prevention and crisis intervention are critical for preventing tragic outcomes. Men's body image and self-esteem can impact their mental health, leading to issues with body dysmorphia and eating disorders.

Men's career and workplace mental health are essential for maintaining job satisfaction and avoiding burnout. Mindfulness practices and spirituality have been shown to improve mental health outcomes for men. Overall, understanding the definition of men's mental health is critical for breaking the stigma and promoting healthy discussions around mental health issues in men.

In conclusion, men's mental health refers to the overall wellbeing of men's emotional, psychological, and social functioning. It encompasses a broad range of mental health conditions, including depression, anxiety, PTSD, trauma, anger management, emotional regulation, addiction, substance abuse, relationship and marriage counseling, stress and burnout prevention, suicide prevention, crisis intervention, body image, self-esteem, career and workplace mental health, spirituality, and mindfulness practices.

Understanding the definition of men's mental health is critical for breaking the stigma and promoting healthy discussions around mental health issues in men.

The Importance of Addressing Men's Mental Health

It's no secret that men face a number of unique challenges when it comes to mental health. From societal pressure to be "tough" and never show weakness, to the expectation that they provide for their families and be the breadwinners, men often find themselves struggling with depression, anxiety, PTSD, anger management, addiction, and more.

Despite these challenges, men are often reluctant to seek help for their mental health issues. They may worry about being stigmatized or judged for seeking help, or they may be unsure of where to turn for assistance.

However, it's important to recognize the importance of addressing men's mental health. When men are struggling with mental health issues, it not only affects them but also their families, relationships, and communities.

Depression and Anxiety in Men

Depression and anxiety are two of the most common mental health issues facing men. Men may be more likely to express their symptoms as anger or irritability, which can make it difficult to identify the underlying problem.

It's important to recognize the signs of depression and anxiety in men, which can include changes in sleep patterns, appetite, and energy levels, as well as feelings of hopelessness and worthlessness.

Men's PTSD and Trauma

Men are more likely than women to experience trauma, such as combat exposure or physical assault. This can lead to the development of PTSD, which can be debilitating if left untreated.

It's important to seek help if you are experiencing symptoms of PTSD, which can include flashbacks, nightmares, and avoidance of triggers.

Men's Anger Management and Emotional Regulation

Men may be more likely to express their emotions through anger, which can be damaging to their relationships and mental health. It's important to learn healthy ways to manage anger and regulate emotions, such as through therapy or mindfulness practices.

Men's Addiction and Substance Abuse

Men are more likely than women to struggle with addiction and substance abuse, which can have serious consequences for their mental and physical health. It's important to seek help if you are struggling with addiction, whether through therapy, support groups, or other resources.

Men's Relationship and Marriage Counseling

Relationships can be a significant source of stress for men, particularly if they are struggling with mental health issues. It's important to seek help if you are experiencing relationship difficulties, whether through individual therapy or couples counseling.

Men's Stress and Burnout Prevention

Men may feel pressure to constantly be working and providing for their families, which can lead to stress and burnout. It's important to take time to prioritize self-care and stress management, such as through exercise, relaxation techniques, and setting healthy boundaries.

Men's Suicide Prevention and Crisis Intervention

Men are more likely than women to die by suicide, making suicide prevention and crisis intervention especially important. It's important to seek help if you are experiencing suicidal thoughts or feelings, whether through a crisis hotline or emergency services.

Men's Body Image and Self-Esteem

Men may also struggle with body image issues and low self-esteem, particularly in relation to societal expectations of masculinity. It's important to prioritize self-care and self-compassion, and to seek help if you are experiencing significant distress related to body image or self-esteem.

Men's Career and Workplace Mental Health

Men may also experience stress and burnout related to their careers and workplace culture. It's important for employers to prioritize mental health in the workplace, and for men to advocate for their own mental health needs and seek support if needed.

Men's Spirituality and Mindfulness Practices

Spirituality and mindfulness practices can be helpful for men in managing stress and promoting mental well-being. It's important to find practices that resonate with you, whether through meditation, yoga, or other spiritual practices.

In conclusion, addressing men's mental health is of utmost importance for the well- being of individuals, families, and communities. It's important to prioritize mental health and seek support when needed, whether through therapy, support groups, or other resources. By breaking the stigma around men's mental health, we can create a culture of openness and support that benefits everyone.

The stigma surrounding men's mental health

The stigma surrounding men's mental health is an unfortunate reality that many men face in the modern world. For years, men have been conditioned to believe that seeking help for mental health issues is a sign of weakness, and they often suffer in silence because of this belief.

Depression and anxiety in men are common mental health disorders that are often overlooked due to the stigma surrounding men's mental health. Men are often expected to be strong and self-reliant, and admitting to struggling with mental health issues can be seen as a sign of weakness. This can lead to men not seeking the help they need and suffering in silence.

Men's PTSD and trauma are also topics that are often stigmatized and not talked about enough. Many men who have experienced trauma or have PTSD feel ashamed to seek help, and this can lead to a host of other issues such as addiction and substance abuse.

Men's anger management and emotional regulation is another area where stigma can be present. Men are often expected to be tough and not show vulnerability, which can make it difficult for them to express their emotions in a healthy way. This can lead to anger issues and difficulty regulating emotions.

Men's addiction and substance abuse are often stigmatized as a moral failing rather than a mental health issue. Men who struggle with addiction may feel ashamed and be hesitant to seek help because of this stigma.

Men's relationship and marriage counseling can also be stigmatized, as it can be seen as an admission of failure or weakness. However, seeking counseling can be a positive step towards improving relationships and mental health.

Men's stress and burnout prevention is an important topic that is often overlooked. Men are often expected to work long hours and put their careers first, which can lead to stress and burnout. However, seeking help and finding ways to manage stress can lead to a healthier and happier life.

Men's suicide prevention and crisis intervention is a topic that is too often stigmatized. Men are at a higher risk of suicide, but may be hesitant to seek help due to the stigma surrounding mental health issues.

Men's body image and self-esteem can also be stigmatized, as men are often expected to be strong and muscular. However, body image issues can lead to mental health issues and seeking help can be a positive step towards improving self-esteem.

Men's career and workplace mental health is an important topic that is often overlooked. Men may feel pressure to succeed in their careers and put their mental health on the backburner. However, seeking help and finding ways to manage stress in the workplace can lead to a happier and healthier life.

Finally, men's spirituality and mindfulness practices may be stigmatized as being too "new age" or "feminine." However, mindfulness practices can be a positive step towards improving mental health and overall well-being.

Breaking the stigma surrounding men's mental health is crucial for improving the lives of men around the world. By acknowledging the stigma and seeking help, men can live happier and healthier lives.

Understanding Men's Mental Health

Common Mental Health Issues in Men

Mental health issues are common in both men and women. However, men are more likely to overlook their mental health concerns due to societal expectations that men should be strong and tough. This can lead to a delay in seeking help, which can exacerbate the symptoms and make it harder to recover. In this chapter, we'll explore the most common mental health issues in men and discuss how you can recognize, manage, and overcome them.

Depression and Anxiety in Men

Depression and anxiety are common mental health issues that affect both men and women. However, men may be less likely to seek help for these conditions due to the stigma surrounding mental health. Symptoms of depression in men may include feelings of sadness, hopelessness, irritability, loss of interest in activities, and physical symptoms such as fatigue, insomnia, or changes in appetite. Anxiety symptoms may include excessive worry, restlessness, difficulty concentrating, and physical symptoms such as sweating, racing heartbeat, or shortness of breath. Men who experience these symptoms should seek professional help.

Men's PTSD and Trauma

PTSD and trauma are common mental health issues that can affect anyone who has experienced a traumatic event. Men who have served in the military, law enforcement, or emergency services may be at a higher risk for PTSD due to their exposure to traumatic events. Symptoms of PTSD may include flashbacks, nightmares, avoidance of triggers, and heightened arousal. Men who experience these symptoms should seek professional help.

Men's Anger Management and Emotional Regulation

Men may struggle with anger management due to societal expectations that men should be tough and aggressive. However, uncontrolled anger can lead to negative consequences such as damaged relationships, legal troubles, and physical health issues. Men who struggle with anger management should seek professional help to learn healthy ways to manage their emotions.

Men's Addiction and Substance Abuse

Substance abuse and addiction can have a significant impact on men's mental health, relationships, and careers. Men may be more likely to engage in risky behaviors such as drug or alcohol abuse due to societal expectations that men should be tough and fearless. Men who struggle with addiction should seek professional help to overcome their substance abuse issues.

Men's Relationship and Marriage Counseling

Men may struggle with relationships due to societal expectations that men should be independent and self-sufficient. However, healthy relationships require vulnerability and emotional intimacy. Men who struggle with relationships should seek professional help to learn healthy communication and relationship skills.

Men's Stress and Burnout Prevention

Stress and burnout can have a significant impact on men's mental health, physical health, and career success. Men may feel pressure to work long hours and achieve success at all costs. However, chronic stress and burnout can lead to physical and mental health issues. Men should prioritize self-care, seek support from loved ones, and seek professional help if needed.

Men's Suicide Prevention and Crisis Intervention

Suicide is a leading cause of death among men. Men may be less likely to seek help for mental health issues due to stigma and societal expectations that men should be strong and tough. However, suicide is preventable. Men who experience suicidal thoughts or behaviors should seek immediate professional help.

Men's Body Image and Self-Esteem

Men may struggle with body image and self-esteem issues due to societal expectations that men should be muscular and physically fit. However, these expectations can be unrealistic and lead to negative self-talk and body dissatisfaction. Men should focus on self-care, body positivity, and seek professional help if needed.

Men's Career and Workplace Mental Health

Men may experience mental health issues related to their careers and workplace due to stress, burnout, and other job-related factors. Men should prioritize self-care, seek support from colleagues, and seek professional help if needed.

Men's Spirituality and Mindfulness Practices

Men may benefit from spirituality and mindfulness practices to improve their mental health and well-being. Mindfulness practices such as meditation, yoga, and deep breathing can help men manage stress and improve their emotional regulation. Men should explore different practices to find what works best for them.

In conclusion, mental health issues are common in men, and seeking help is a sign of strength, not weakness. Men should prioritize their mental health, seek professional help when needed, and work to break the stigma surrounding men's mental health.

Depression and Anxiety

Depression and anxiety are two of the most common mental health issues that affect men worldwide. Depression is a mood disorder characterized by feelings of sadness, hopelessness, and a loss of interest in activities that were once pleasurable. Anxiety, on the other hand, is a condition that causes excessive worry, fear, and nervousness. While these two mental health problems are different, they often occur together and can significantly impact a man's quality of life.

Depression and anxiety can have a wide range of causes, including genetics, life events, and biochemical imbalances in the brain. Men who experience depression or anxiety may feel ashamed or embarrassed about their symptoms, which can prevent them from seeking help. However, it's important to remember that experiencing depression or anxiety is not a sign of weakness, and seeking help is a brave and necessary step towards recovery.

If you're experiencing depression or anxiety, there are many options for treatment. Psychotherapy, medications, and lifestyle changes can all be effective in managing symptoms. Cognitive-behavioral therapy (CBT) is a type of psychotherapy that is often used to treat depression and anxiety. CBT helps men identify negative thought patterns and learn new skills to manage their symptoms.

In addition to therapy, medications such as antidepressants and anti-anxiety medications can be helpful in managing symptoms. However, it's important to note that not all medications are effective for everyone, and there can be side effects.

Lifestyle changes such as regular exercise, healthy eating, and stress management techniques like meditation and mindfulness can also be helpful in managing depression and anxiety. Regular exercise has been shown to release endorphins, which are natural mood-boosters. Eating a healthy diet can also help improve mood and energy levels. Mindfulness practices like meditation and deep breathing exercises can help reduce stress and promote relaxation.

If you're experiencing depression or anxiety, it's important to seek help as soon as possible. With the right treatment and support, it is possible to manage these conditions and improve your quality of life. Remember, seeking help is not a sign of weakness, but a brave and necessary step towards recovery.

PTSD and trauma

PTSD and trauma are two of the most debilitating mental health conditions that can affect men. PTSD, or post-traumatic stress disorder, is a mental health condition that develops in people who have experienced or witnessed a traumatic event. Trauma, on the other hand, refers to an emotional response to a distressing event that overwhelms a person's ability to cope.

PTSD and trauma can have a significant impact on a man's mental health, leading to symptoms such as flashbacks, nightmares, anxiety, depression, and anger. Men who have experienced trauma or have been diagnosed with PTSD may also struggle with substance abuse, relationship problems, and difficulties at work.

It is essential for men to seek help if they are experiencing symptoms of PTSD or trauma. Counseling, therapy, and medication can help manage symptoms and improve mental health. Men's mental health professionals can also provide support and guidance on anger management and emotional regulation, addiction and substance abuse, relationship and marriage counseling, stress and burnout prevention, and suicide prevention and crisis intervention.

It is important to note that men may be less likely to seek help for mental health conditions such as PTSD and trauma due to societal expectations of masculinity. However, seeking help is a sign of strength and can lead to improved mental health and overall well-being.

In addition to seeking professional help, men can also practice mindfulness and spirituality to manage symptoms of PTSD and trauma. Mindfulness practices such as meditation and breathing exercises can help reduce stress and anxiety, while spirituality can provide a sense of meaning and purpose.

Breaking the stigma surrounding men's mental health is essential in encouraging men to seek help for conditions such as PTSD and trauma. By prioritizing mental health and seeking help when needed, men can improve their overall well-being and lead fulfilling lives.

Anger management and emotional regulation

Anger is a natural human emotion that we all experience at some point. However, when anger is not managed correctly, it can lead to negative consequences such as aggression, violence, and damage to relationships. Therefore, it is important to learn how to regulate emotions and manage anger effectively.

Anger management is the process of recognizing and understanding anger triggers, learning to control emotional reactions, and developing healthy coping mechanisms. Emotional regulation, on the other hand, is the ability to manage and control one's emotions in a healthy and positive way.

In men's mental health, anger management and emotional regulation are critical skills to develop. Men may face unique challenges that can trigger anger, such as societal expectations of masculinity, relationship issues, and work-related stress. Additionally, men may be more prone to bottling up emotions and not seeking help, which can exacerbate anger and other mental health issues.

To manage anger and regulate emotions effectively, it is important to identify triggers and learn coping strategies. Some effective strategies include deep breathing exercises, progressive muscle relaxation, and mindfulness practices. It is also important to communicate effectively and assertively, to avoid bottling up emotions and to express oneself in a healthy and constructive way.

In some cases, anger and emotional regulation issues may require professional help. This can include therapy, counseling, or medication. Seeking help is a sign of strength and can lead to improved mental health and overall well-being.

In conclusion, anger management and emotional regulation are essential skills for men's mental health. By learning to recognize triggers, develop healthy coping mechanisms, and seek help when necessary, men can improve their mental health and relationships. Remember, it is okay to ask for help and take steps towards a healthier and happier life.

Addiction and substance abuse

Factors that Contribute to Men's Mental Health Issues

Mental health issues are a growing concern in the modern world, affecting men of all ages, races, and backgrounds. While mental health issues are often stigmatized and overlooked, it is important to recognize the factors that contribute to men's mental health issues. By understanding these factors, men can take proactive steps to protect their mental health and seek the necessary support.

Depression and Anxiety in Men

Depression and anxiety are two of the most common mental health issues that affect men. These conditions can be caused by a variety of factors, including genetics, life events, and chemical imbalances in the brain. Men may be more likely to experience depression and anxiety due to societal pressures to be strong and self-sufficient, which can make it difficult to ask for help.

Men's PTSD and Trauma

Post-traumatic stress disorder (PTSD) and trauma are common mental health issues that affect men who have experienced traumatic events such as military combat, sexual assault, or domestic violence. Men may be more likely to develop PTSD and trauma due to societal expectations to be tough and resilient, which can make it difficult to seek help and support.

Men's Anger Management and Emotional Regulation

Anger and emotional regulation issues are common among men, who may feel pressure to suppress their emotions and appear tough and in control. This can lead to unhealthy coping mechanisms such as substance abuse or aggression, which can further exacerbate mental health issues.

Men's Addiction and Substance Abuse

Addiction and substance abuse are common mental health issues that affect men, often as a result of stress, trauma, and other underlying mental health issues. Men may be more likely to develop addiction and substance abuse due to societal expectations to be self-sufficient and resilient, which can make it difficult to seek help.

Men's Relationship and Marriage Counseling

Relationship and marriage issues can have a significant impact on men's mental health, particularly if there are underlying mental health issues or communication problems.

Men may be more likely to struggle with relationship issues due to societal expectations to be providers and protectors, which can make it difficult to seek help and support.

Men's Stress and Burnout Prevention

Stress and burnout are common mental health issues that affect men in the workplace and at home. Men may be more likely to experience stress and burnout due to societal expectations to be successful and ambitious, which can make it difficult to take time for self-care and relaxation.

Men's Suicide Prevention and Crisis Intervention

Suicide is a major concern for men's mental health, with men being more likely to die by suicide than women. This may be due to societal expectations to be strong and self- sufficient, which can make it difficult to seek help and support during times of crisis.

Men's Body Image and Self-Esteem

Body image and self-esteem issues are common among men, who may feel pressure to conform to societal expectations of masculinity and physical appearance. This can lead to unhealthy behaviors such as excessive exercise or restrictive eating, which can further exacerbate mental health issues.

Men's Career and Workplace Mental Health

Workplace stress and burnout can have a significant impact on men's mental health, particularly if there are underlying mental health issues or communication problems. Men may be more likely to struggle with career and workplace issues due to societal expectations to be successful and ambitious, which can make it difficult to take time for self-care and relaxation.

Men's Spirituality and Mindfulness Practices

Spirituality and mindfulness practices can be powerful tools for men's mental health, helping to reduce stress, improve self-awareness, and promote emotional regulation. Men may be more likely to benefit from these practices due to societal expectations to be self-sufficient and in control, which can make it difficult to seek help and support.

Societal expectations and gender roles

Societal expectations and gender roles have a significant impact on men's mental health. From a young age, boys are often taught to suppress their emotions and adopt a "tough" demeanor. This can lead to a sense of isolation and feelings of inadequacy when they are unable to live up to these expectations.

Gender roles can also create harmful stereotypes that limit men's emotional expression and prevent them from seeking help when they need it. Men are often expected to be the primary breadwinners, leaders, and protectors of their families, which can create a sense of pressure and stress that can lead to mental health issues such as depression and anxiety.

Men who experience trauma or PTSD may feel even more pressure to suppress their emotions and "tough it out," leading to further emotional distress and potentially harmful coping mechanisms like substance abuse or anger outbursts.

Additionally, societal expectations can impact men's relationships and self-esteem. Men may feel pressure to conform to societal ideals of masculinity, including having a certain body type or level of success, which can lead to feelings of shame or inadequacy when they are unable to meet these expectations.

It's important for men to recognize the impact of societal expectations and gender roles on their mental health and seek help when needed. This may involve challenging harmful stereotypes and expectations, learning healthy coping mechanisms, and seeking support from friends, family, or mental health professionals.

Breaking the stigma surrounding men's mental health is crucial in creating a more supportive and understanding society. By promoting open communication, empathy, and acceptance, we can work towards a world where all men feel comfortable seeking help for their mental health concerns without fear of judgment or shame.

Childhood experiences and upbringing

Childhood experiences and upbringing play a significant role in shaping a person's mental health and overall well-being. Many men who struggle with mental health issues often trace the root cause of their problems to their childhood experiences. Childhood events such as abuse, neglect, bullying, and traumatic experiences can have a lasting impact on an individual's mental health and emotional stability.

Many men who experience childhood trauma or adverse childhood experiences (ACEs) are at higher risk of developing mental health conditions such as depression, anxiety, PTSD, and addiction. It is crucial to understand that childhood experiences can have a profound impact on the way men perceive themselves, others, and the world around them.

Men who experienced abuse or neglect as children may struggle with issues such as trust, intimacy, and emotional regulation. Men who grew up in households where anger and aggression were prevalent may have difficulty managing their own anger and emotions, which can lead to outbursts and destructive behavior.

It is essential for men to address their childhood experiences and upbringing as part of their mental health journey. Therapy and counseling can help men process their childhood trauma and develop healthy coping mechanisms that promote emotional healing and growth. Additionally, mindfulness practices such as meditation and yoga can help men cultivate self-awareness, emotional regulation, and stress management skills.

As men work through their childhood experiences and upbringing, it is important to remember that healing is a process. It takes time, patience, and effort to overcome the negative impact of childhood trauma and develop a healthy sense of self-worth and emotional stability. However, with the right support and resources, men can break the stigma surrounding mental health and embark on a journey of healing and recovery.

Physical health and lifestyle choices

Physical health and lifestyle choices are critical factors that impact men's mental health. Many studies have shown that maintaining a healthy lifestyle can improve mood, reduce stress and anxiety, and boost self-esteem. On the other hand, unhealthy habits such as smoking, excessive drinking, poor diet, and lack of exercise can lead to physical and mental health problems.

Depression and anxiety in men can often be linked to unhealthy lifestyle choices. A sedentary lifestyle, poor sleep habits, and excessive alcohol and drug use can all contribute to these mental health conditions. By making healthier choices such as exercising regularly, eating a balanced diet, and getting enough sleep, men can reduce their risk of developing depression and anxiety.

Men's PTSD and trauma can also be affected by their lifestyle choices. Many people who suffer from PTSD turn to alcohol or drugs as a way to cope with their symptoms. However, this can lead to addiction and further exacerbate the problem. It is important for men to seek out healthy coping mechanisms such as therapy, meditation, and exercise to manage their symptoms.

Anger management and emotional regulation are also linked to physical health. Exercise has been shown to be an effective way to manage anger and reduce stress. Men who struggle with anger issues can also benefit from practices such as mindfulness and meditation.

Men's addiction and substance abuse are often linked to underlying mental health issues. It is crucial for men to seek professional help and support to overcome addiction and develop healthy coping mechanisms.

Men's relationship and marriage counseling can also be impacted by physical health. A healthy relationship requires both partners to maintain good physical and mental health. By prioritizing healthy lifestyle choices, men can improve their relationships and strengthen their emotional bonds with their partners.

Stress and burnout prevention are essential for men's mental health. Exercise, healthy eating habits, and mindfulness practices can all help reduce stress and prevent burnout.

Men's suicide prevention and crisis intervention can also be impacted by physical health. Men who struggle with mental health issues may turn to suicidal thoughts as a way to cope. By prioritizing healthy lifestyle choices, men can reduce their risk of suicide and seek out the support they need to heal.

Men's body image and self-esteem can also be affected by physical health. Exercise and a healthy diet can help men feel better about their bodies and boost their self-esteem.

Finally, men's career and workplace mental health can also be impacted by their physical health. A healthy lifestyle can help men manage stress and achieve a better work-life balance, leading to increased job satisfaction and productivity.

In conclusion, physical health and lifestyle choices are critical factors that impact men's mental health. By prioritizing healthy habits such as exercise, good sleep habits, healthy eating, and mindfulness practices, men can improve their mental health and overall wellbeing. Seeking professional help and support is also crucial for men who struggle with mental health issues.

Seeking Help and Support

Barriers to Seeking Help

Despite the growing awareness of mental health issues, many men still struggle to seek help when they need it. There are several reasons for this, and understanding these barriers can help men overcome them and take steps towards better mental health.

Stigma and Shame

One of the biggest barriers to seeking help for mental health issues is the stigma and shame that still surrounds mental illness in many cultures. Men may feel that admitting to struggling with their mental health makes them appear weak or inadequate, or that seeking therapy or medication is a sign of failure. This can be particularly true for men who hold traditional ideas about masculinity and the need to be self-reliant.

Lack of Awareness

Another barrier to seeking help for mental health issues is a lack of awareness. Men may not recognize the signs and symptoms of mental illness, or they may dismiss their own struggles as something they can handle on their own. This can be especially true for men who are used to pushing through challenges or who have a high tolerance for stress.

Access to Care

Another barrier to seeking help for mental health issues is a lack of access to care. Men may live in areas where mental health services are scarce or unaffordable, or they may not have health insurance that covers mental health care. This can be particularly true for men who are self-employed or who work in industries that do not provide health benefits.

Fear of Discrimination

Another barrier to seeking help for mental health issues is a fear of discrimination. Men who belong to marginalized groups, such as racial or ethnic minorities, may worry that their mental health struggles will be dismissed or stigmatized by healthcare providers. This can be particularly true for men who have experienced discrimination or trauma in the past.

Breaking the Stigma

Breaking the stigma around mental health is essential for men to seek help and improve their mental health. It is important to prioritize mental health and seek help when needed, while also encouraging others to do the same. Men should know that seeking help is a sign of strength, not weakness, and that mental health care is just as important as physical health care.

Increasing awareness of mental health issues and improving access to care can also make a significant difference in breaking down these barriers. Men's mental health should be a priority for healthcare providers, employers, and policymakers, and efforts should be made to ensure that all men have access to high-quality mental health care.

In conclusion, there are several barriers to seeking help for mental health issues that men face. However, by breaking down the stigma, increasing awareness, improving access to care, and creating safe and supportive environments, men can take steps towards better mental health and well-being.

Overcoming the Stigma

One of the biggest challenges that men face when it comes to mental health is the stigma that surrounds it. For generations, men have been taught to be strong and not show weakness or vulnerability. This attitude has led to a culture where mental health issues are seen as a sign of weakness, and seeking help is seen as a failure.

However, it's important to remember that mental health issues are just like any other health issue, and there is no shame in seeking help when you need it. Overcoming the stigma surrounding mental health is crucial for men to get the help they need and lead healthy, fulfilling lives.

One way to overcome the stigma is to educate yourself and others about mental health. This can involve learning about the different types of mental health issues, their symptoms, and treatment options. It can also involve talking openly about mental health with friends, family, and colleagues. By discussing mental health openly and honestly, we can break down the barriers that prevent men from seeking help.

Another way to overcome the stigma is to seek out support groups or therapy. These resources can provide a safe and supportive environment where men can talk about their feelings and struggles without fear of judgment. By connecting with others who have similar experiences, men can find comfort and understanding, which can help to reduce feelings of isolation and shame.

It's also important to remember that seeking help for mental health issues is a sign of strength, not weakness. Asking for help takes courage, and it shows that you are taking control of your life and making positive changes. By seeking help, men can learn coping skills and strategies that can help them manage their symptoms and live happier, healthier lives.

In conclusion, overcoming the stigma surrounding mental health is essential for men to get the help they need and lead fulfilling lives. By educating ourselves and others about mental health, seeking out support groups and therapy, and remembering that seeking help is a sign of strength, not weakness, men can break down the barriers that prevent them from seeking help and live their best lives.

Types of treatment and support available

When it comes to treating mental health issues, there isn't a one-size-fits-all solution. The type of treatment and support needed will vary depending on the individual, their mental health condition, and their personal preferences. In this chapter, we will explore some of the different types of treatment and support available for men's mental health.

Therapy

Therapy is a popular treatment option for mental health issues. It involves talking to a mental health professional, such as a psychologist or therapist, about your problems and concerns. Therapy can help you develop coping skills, change negative thought patterns, and improve your overall mental health. There are several different types of therapy, including cognitive-behavioral therapy, which focuses on changing negative thought patterns, and interpersonal therapy, which focuses on improving communication and relationships.

Medication

Medication can be a useful tool for managing mental health conditions such as depression, anxiety, and PTSD. There are several different types of medication available, including antidepressants, anti-anxiety medication, and mood stabilizers.

It's important to work closely with a doctor or psychiatrist when taking medication, as some medications can have side effects and interact with other medications.

Support Groups

Support groups are a great way to connect with others who are going through similar struggles. They provide a safe and supportive environment where men can share their experiences and learn from others. Support groups can be found online or in person and can cover a wide range of topics, including addiction, anxiety, and PTSD.

Alternative Therapies

Alternative therapies, such as yoga, mindfulness practices, and acupuncture, can be useful for managing mental health issues and improving overall wellbeing. These therapies focus on reducing stress and promoting relaxation, which can be beneficial for men who are struggling with anxiety, depression, or PTSD.

In conclusion, there are many different types of treatment and support available for men's mental health. It's important to work with a mental health professional to find the right treatment plan for your specific needs and preferences. Remember, seeking help is a sign of strength, and there is no shame in asking for support when you need it.

Counseling and therapy

Counseling and therapy are powerful tools that men can use to address their mental health concerns. Unfortunately, there is still a stigma surrounding therapy, which can discourage men from seeking help. However, counseling and therapy can provide a safe and supportive space for men to explore their emotions, develop coping skills, and improve their mental well-being.

Depression and anxiety are common mental health concerns that affect many men. Counseling and therapy can help men understand the root causes of their depression and anxiety, develop coping skills, and learn strategies to manage their symptoms.

Additionally, therapy can help men identify and address any underlying issues that may be contributing to their depression and anxiety, such as trauma or relationship problems.

Men's PTSD and trauma can be debilitating and can significantly impact their quality of life. Counseling and therapy can provide a safe and supportive environment for men to process their trauma and develop coping skills. Therapists can help men identify triggers and develop strategies to manage their symptoms, such as grounding techniques.

Anger management and emotional regulation are essential skills for men to develop to improve their mental health and relationships. Counseling and therapy can help men identify the underlying causes of their anger and develop strategies to manage their emotions in healthy ways. Therapists can also help men develop communication skills to express their emotions in constructive ways.

Men's addiction and substance abuse can be challenging to overcome without professional help. Counseling and therapy can provide men with the support and guidance they need to overcome their addiction. Therapists can help men identify the underlying causes of their addiction and develop strategies to manage their cravings and triggers.

Men's relationship and marriage counseling can help men improve their communication skills, develop healthy boundaries, and address any underlying issues that may be impacting their relationships. Counseling and therapy can provide a safe space for men to explore their emotions and develop strategies to improve their relationships.

Men's stress and burnout prevention are essential for maintaining good mental health and preventing burnout. Counseling and therapy can help men develop coping skills, identify stressors, and develop strategies to manage their stress in healthy ways.

Therapists can also help men identify areas in their lives that may be contributing to their stress and develop strategies to manage these areas more effectively.

Men's suicide prevention and crisis intervention are critical for supporting men who may be struggling with suicidal thoughts or experiencing a mental health crisis. Counseling and therapy can provide men with the support and guidance they need to manage their mental health and prevent suicide. Therapists can also help men identify warning signs and develop strategies to manage their mental health more effectively.

Men's body image and self-esteem can be impacted by societal pressures to conform to certain beauty standards. Counseling and therapy can provide men with the support and guidance they need to improve their body image and self-esteem. Therapists can help men identify the underlying causes of their negative body image and develop strategies to improve their self-esteem.

Men's career and workplace mental health are important for maintaining good mental health and preventing burnout. Counseling and therapy can help men develop coping skills, manage stress, and improve their communication skills in the workplace. Therapists can also help men identify areas in their careers that may be contributing to their stress and develop strategies to manage these areas more effectively.

Men's spirituality and mindfulness practices can be powerful tools for improving mental health and well-being. Counseling and therapy can provide men with the support and guidance they need to develop their spirituality and mindfulness practices. Therapists can help men identify practices that align with their values and beliefs and develop strategies to integrate these practices into their daily lives.

In conclusion, counseling and therapy are powerful tools that men can use to improve their mental health and well-being. Whether men are struggling with depression and anxiety, PTSD and trauma, anger management and emotional regulation, addiction and substance abuse, relationship and marriage issues, stress and burnout, suicidal thoughts, body image and self-esteem, career and workplace issues, or spirituality and mindfulness practices, counseling and therapy can provide the support and guidance they need to manage these concerns effectively. Despite the stigma surrounding therapy, men should not hesitate to seek help from a qualified mental health professional when they need it.

Medication

Medication is a common treatment option for men who are struggling with mental health issues such as depression, anxiety, PTSD, anger management, addiction, and more. While medication can be highly effective in treating these conditions, it's important to recognize that it is not a cure-all solution. Medication should always be used in conjunction with other therapies and lifestyle changes to achieve lasting results.

If you are considering medication for your mental health, it's important to work with a qualified healthcare professional who can help you determine the best course of treatment. This may include a psychiatric evaluation, blood tests, and a review of your medical history. Your doctor will also work with you to identify any potential side effects and develop a plan for monitoring your progress.

One of the most common types of medication used to treat mental health conditions is antidepressants. These medications work by increasing the levels of certain chemicals in the brain that regulate mood. While antidepressants can be highly effective, they can also take several weeks to start working and may cause side effects such as nausea, insomnia, and weight gain.

Another type of medication that may be used to manage mental health conditions is antipsychotics. These medications can help to reduce the severity of symptoms such as hallucinations and delusions, which are commonly experienced by men with conditions such as schizophrenia and bipolar disorder. However, antipsychotics can also cause side effects such as weight gain, drowsiness, and tremors.

Other types of medication that may be used to treat mental health conditions include mood stabilizers, anti-anxiety medications, and stimulants. These medications can be highly effective in managing symptoms, but it's important to work closely with your doctor to ensure that you are taking the right medication at the right dosage.

In addition to medication, it's important to prioritize lifestyle changes such as exercise, a healthy diet, and stress management techniques to support your mental health. With the right combination of medication and lifestyle changes, men can achieve lasting relief from mental health conditions and improve their overall well-being.

Support groups

Support Groups: A Powerful Tool for Men's Mental Health

When facing mental health challenges such as depression, anxiety, PTSD, addiction, or anger management issues, it's easy to feel isolated, overwhelmed, and hopeless. Men tend to struggle with asking for help or showing vulnerability, which can make their journey towards recovery even more challenging. However, support groups can be a game-changer for men's mental health, providing a safe and supportive environment to share experiences, learn from others, and find hope and inspiration.

What are Support Groups?

Support groups are gatherings of people who share a common problem, condition, or experience and want to help each other cope, heal, and grow. Support groups can be led by a mental health professional, a peer, or a volunteer and can take various forms, from in- person meetings to online forums, chat rooms, or phone calls. Some support groups have a specific focus, such as addiction recovery or PTSD, while others can be more general, offering a space for men to talk about their mental health challenges and find comfort and understanding.

How Can Support Groups Help Men's Mental Health?

Support groups are not a substitute for professional therapy or medication, but they can complement these treatments and provide additional benefits, such as:

- Reducing isolation and loneliness: Men often feel that they are the only ones struggling with mental health issues, which can reinforce the stigma and shame associated with these conditions. Support groups provide a sense of community and belonging, showing men that they are not alone and that others have similar struggles.

- Encouraging sharing and communication: Men can be reluctant to open up about their emotions or vulnerabilities, especially in front of strangers. Support groups provide a non- judgmental and safe space where men can express their feelings, thoughts, and concerns without fear of being ridiculed or criticized.

- Providing practical advice and tips: Support groups can offer practical strategies, coping skills, and resources for managing mental health challenges, such as meditation, exercise, or self-care practices. Men can also learn from others' experiences and perspectives, gaining new insights and ideas.

- Boosting self-esteem and confidence: Participating in a support group can be a powerful confidence booster, as men can see their progress, share their successes, and receive recognition and encouragement from others. Support groups can also help men challenge negative beliefs and self-talk, replacing them with more positive and empowering ones.

How to Find and Join a Support Group?

If you're interested in joining a support group, there are several ways to find one that suits your needs and preferences:

- Ask your therapist or mental health provider for recommendations or referrals.

- Search online for support groups in your area or for specific mental health conditions.

- Check with local hospitals, community centers, or religious organizations that may offer support groups.

- Ask friends or family members if they know of any support groups or if they would be interested in creating one together.

- Consider joining an online support group, especially if you live in a remote area or have mobility or transportation issues.

Support groups can be a valuable tool for men's mental health, providing a safe and supportive space to share, learn, and grow. If you're struggling with mental health challenges, consider joining a support group and see how it can make a difference in your life.

Remember, seeking help is a sign of strength, not weakness, and you deserve to live a happy and healthy life.

Self-help strategies

Self-help strategies are an essential aspect of mental health management. For men struggling with depression, anxiety, PTSD, trauma, anger management, addiction, relationship issues, stress, burnout, suicidal thoughts, body image, self-esteem, career, and workplace-related mental challenges, self-help strategies can be a lifeline. Here are some self-help strategies that can help you manage your mental health and well-being.

Firstly, practice mindfulness. Mindfulness involves being present in the moment and paying attention to your thoughts, feelings, and surroundings. Mindfulness can help you manage stress, anxiety, and depression by allowing you to focus on the present and reduce negative self-talk.

Secondly, exercise regularly. Exercise is a powerful mood booster that can help alleviate symptoms of depression and anxiety. Exercise releases endorphins, which are the body's natural mood-boosting chemicals. Regular exercise can also help improve sleep quality, which is essential for mental well-being.

Thirdly, practice self-care. Self-care involves taking care of yourself physically, emotionally, and mentally. Self-care can include activities such as taking a relaxing bath, reading a book, spending time in nature, or doing something creative.

Fourthly, talk to someone. Talking to someone about your feelings can be a powerful tool for managing mental health challenges. This can be a friend, family member, or mental health professional. It's essential to reach out for help when you need it.

Finally, practice gratitude. Gratitude involves focusing on the positive aspects of your life and being thankful for what you have. Practicing gratitude can help shift your focus from negative thoughts and emotions to positive ones, which can improve your mental health and well-being.

In conclusion, self-help strategies can be an essential tool for managing mental health challenges. By practicing mindfulness, exercising regularly, practicing self-care, talking to someone, and practicing gratitude, you can take control of your mental health and well- being. Remember, it's okay to ask for help when you need it.

Specific Issues and Approaches

Men's Relationship and Marriage Counseling

Relationships and marriages can be both rewarding and challenging. Men often find it difficult to express their emotions and communicate effectively with their partners, leading to breakdowns in their relationships. This can cause feelings of isolation, depression, and anxiety, further exacerbating existing mental health issues.

Relationship and marriage counseling can be an effective tool for men to address these issues and improve their mental health. It provides a safe and confidential space for men to explore their emotions, learn effective communication skills, and develop strategies to improve their relationships.

In counseling, men can learn to identify their emotions, express them in a healthy manner, and understand their partner's perspective. The counselor can also help men develop coping mechanisms to deal with stress and conflict, and work through trauma or past experiences that may affect their relationships.

Counseling can also help men to understand the underlying issues that may be causing problems in their relationships, such as addiction, infidelity, or mental health issues. By addressing these issues, men can begin to rebuild trust with their partners and improve their overall mental health and well-being.

It is important for men to understand that seeking counseling does not make them weak or less of a man. It takes courage and strength to acknowledge and address their problems, and counseling can be a valuable tool in their journey towards better mental health.

In conclusion, men's relationship and marriage counseling can be a crucial step towards improving their mental health and well-being. It can provide a safe and confidential space for men to explore their emotions, learn effective communication skills, and develop strategies to improve their relationships. By seeking counseling, men can begin to rebuild trust with their partners, address underlying issues, and improve their overall mental health. It is important for men to understand that seeking help is a sign of strength and courage, and that they do not have to face their problems alone.

Communication and conflict resolution

Communication and conflict resolution are two of the most essential skills that men need to develop to maintain their mental health. Conflicts are a natural part of life, and they can occur in any situation, whether it is at home, work, or personal relationships. Communication plays a significant role in how we deal with these conflicts.

As a man, it is important to learn how to communicate effectively, especially when you are dealing with depression, anxiety, PTSD, or trauma. These conditions can make it difficult for you to express yourself in a healthy and productive way. However, with practice and guidance, you can learn to communicate your thoughts and feelings effectively.

One of the key aspects of effective communication is active listening. This means that you need to listen to the other person's perspective and try to understand their point of view. When you actively listen, you show that you respect the other person's feelings and opinions, and this can help to build trust and understanding.

Another important aspect of communication is conflict resolution. When conflicts arise, it is important to approach them with a calm and rational mindset. This means that you need to avoid getting defensive or aggressive, and instead focus on finding a solution that works for both parties.

To achieve conflict resolution, you need to be willing to compromise and negotiate. This means that you need to be open to other perspectives and be willing to find a solution that works for everyone involved. By being flexible and open-minded, you can develop stronger relationships and avoid unnecessary conflicts.

In addition to communication and conflict resolution, men also need to learn how to manage their anger and regulate their emotions. Anger can be a powerful emotion, and if not managed properly, it can lead to destructive behavior and negative consequences.

Men can learn to manage their anger and regulate their emotions by practicing mindfulness and other relaxation techniques. These practices can help to reduce stress and anxiety, improve mood and increase overall well-being.

In conclusion, communication and conflict resolution are essential skills that men need to develop to maintain their mental health. By practicing active listening, conflict resolution, anger management, and emotional regulation, men can build stronger relationships, reduce stress and anxiety, and improve overall well-being.

Intimacy and sexual health

Intimacy and Sexual Health: Navigating the Challenges of Men's Mental Health

Intimacy and sexual health can be sensitive topics for many men, especially those struggling with mental health issues like depression, anxiety, PTSD, addiction, or relationship problems. These issues can affect a man's libido, sexual performance, self-esteem, and ability to connect emotionally with their partner or find pleasure in sex. In this subchapter, we'll explore some of the common challenges men face in the realm of intimacy and sexual health and offer some tips and resources for improving your sexual well-being and mental health.

Depression and Anxiety in Men: How They Affect Your Sex Life

Depression and anxiety are two of the most common mental health issues that can affect men's sexual health. Both conditions can decrease your sex drive, cause erectile dysfunction or premature ejaculation, and make it harder to enjoy sex or feel connected to your partner emotionally. If you're struggling with depression or anxiety, it's important to talk to your doctor or mental health provider about treatment options that can help alleviate your symptoms and improve your sexual function. Some strategies that may help include:

- Cognitive-behavioral therapy (CBT) to address negative thoughts, beliefs, and behaviors that contribute to your depression or anxiety

- Medications like selective serotonin reuptake inhibitors (SSRIs) or serotonin- norepinephrine reuptake inhibitors (SNRIs) that can improve your mood and reduce anxiety

- Lifestyle changes like exercise, healthy eating, and stress management techniques that can boost your energy, mood, and self-esteem.

PTSD and Trauma: Healing Your Wounds and Reconnecting with Your Body

If you've experienced trauma or have PTSD, you may struggle with intimacy and sexual health issues like avoidance, hypervigilance, flashbacks, or dissociation. Trauma can make it hard to trust others, feel safe and comfortable in your body, or enjoy sex without being triggered by memories or sensations related to your trauma. If you're struggling with PTSD or trauma-related issues, it's important to seek professional help from a therapist or trauma specialist who can help you process your experiences, manage your symptoms, and develop coping strategies that can help you feel more in control of your body and your sexual experiences. Some possible treatments for trauma-related sexual issues include:

- Trauma-focused therapy like Eye Movement Desensitization and Reprocessing (EMDR) or Prolonged Exposure Therapy (PE) that can help you process traumatic memories and reduce your physiological arousal

- Mindfulness-based practices like meditation, yoga, or deep breathing that can help you calm your nervous system and reconnect with your body in a safe, nonjudgmental way

- Sensate focus exercises or other guided sex therapy techniques that can help you learn to communicate your needs and desires, explore your body in a gradual and comfortable way, and build intimacy and pleasure with your partner.

Addiction and Substance Abuse: Breaking the Cycle and Rebuilding Your Relationships

Addiction and substance abuse can have a devastating impact on your sexual health and intimacy, as well as your mental and physical well-being. If you're struggling with addiction or substance abuse, it's important to seek help from a qualified treatment provider who can help you detox, manage your withdrawal symptoms, and develop a recovery plan that addresses your underlying mental health issues, relationship problems, or trauma history. Some strategies that may be helpful for addiction-related sexual issues include:

- Group therapy or support groups like Alcoholics Anonymous, Narcotics Anonymous, or Sex Addicts Anonymous that can provide peer support, accountability, and education on healthy sexual behaviors

- Cognitive-behavioral therapy (CBT) or other evidence-based therapies that can help you identify and challenge the thoughts, beliefs, and behaviors that contribute to your addiction or sexual dysfunction

- Couples or family therapy that can help you rebuild trust, communication, and intimacy with your partner or loved ones and address any unresolved emotional issues that may be contributing to your addiction or sexual issues.

Relationships and Marriage Counseling: Improving Communication, Trust, and Intimacy

Relationships and marriage can be a source of joy and fulfillment, but they can also be a source of stress, conflict, and emotional pain, especially if you're struggling with mental health issues like depression, anxiety, trauma, or addiction. If you're experiencing relationship or intimacy problems, it's important to seek professional help from a licensed therapist or relationship counselor who can help you and your partner explore your feelings, needs, and expectations, and develop a plan for improving your communication, trust, and intimacy. Some possible strategies for improving your relationship and sexual health include:

- Learning to communicate assertively, empathetically, and non-judgmentally with your partner, and practicing active listening and validation skills

- Building emotional intimacy through shared activities, vulnerability, and touch, and exploring new ways of expressing affection and love

- Addressing any unresolved issues or conflicts that may be contributing to your relationship problems, and developing a plan for resolving them in a healthy, constructive way.

Stress and Burnout Prevention: Prioritizing Self-Care and Pleasure

Stress and burnout can take a toll on your mental and physical health, as well as your sexual well-being and relationship satisfaction. If you're feeling overwhelmed, exhausted, or disconnected from your body and your partner, it's important to prioritize self-care and pleasure as a way of reducing stress and boosting your mood, energy, and libido. Some possible self-care and pleasure strategies that may be helpful include:

- Practicing mindfulness-based techniques like meditation, yoga, or deep breathing that can help you relax, refocus, and tune into your body and your senses

- Engaging in physical activities that you enjoy, like exercise, dancing, or sports, that can help you release tension, increase endorphins, and improve your sexual function and confidence

- Exploring new ways of experiencing pleasure and intimacy with yourself and your partner, like erotic massage, sensual touch, or fantasy play, that can help you feel more connected, relaxed, and fulfilled sexually.

Suicide Prevention and Crisis Intervention: Seeking Help When You Need It Most

If you're struggling with mental health issues like depression, anxiety, trauma, addiction, or relationship problems, it's important to know that you're not alone and that help is available. If you're feeling hopeless, helpless, or suicidal, it's vital to seek immediate help from a mental health provider, crisis hotline, or emergency department. Some resources that may be helpful in a crisis include:

- National Suicide Prevention Lifeline: 1-800-273-TALK (8255)

- Crisis Text Line: Text HOME to 741741

- SAMHSA National Helpline: 1-800-662-HELP (4357)

- Veterans Crisis Line: 1-800-273-8255, Press 1.

Remember, seeking help is a sign of strength, not weakness, and there is no shame in asking for support when you need it most. Whether you're struggling with intimacy and sexual health issues, addiction, trauma, or other mental health challenges, there is hope for healing, recovery, and a fulfilling, joyful life.

Infidelity and Trust Issues

Infidelity and trust issues are a common problem in relationships and can have a significant impact on men's mental health. Infidelity refers to the act of being unfaithful to a partner by engaging in sexual or emotional relationships with someone else. Trust issues arise when one partner feels that the other is not trustworthy or reliable.

Infidelity can lead to feelings of betrayal, anger, and hurt. Men who have been cheated on may experience depression and anxiety, and they may struggle with self-esteem and trust in future relationships. Infidelity can also lead to problems with anger management and emotional regulation, as men may struggle to control their emotions in the wake of such a traumatic experience.

Trust issues can be equally damaging to men's mental health. When a partner feels that their significant other is not trustworthy, it can create a sense of insecurity and anxiety. Men who struggle with trust issues may find it difficult to form meaningful relationships and may experience feelings of isolation and loneliness.

Dealing with infidelity and trust issues requires a willingness to communicate openly and honestly with your partner. Couples therapy can be an effective way to address these issues and can help men develop the skills they need to rebuild trust and repair their relationships.

In addition to seeking professional help, men can take steps to improve their mental health and well-being by practicing self-care, mindfulness, and stress management techniques. These practices can help men develop the resilience and emotional regulation skills they need to navigate the challenges of infidelity and trust issues.

Ultimately, overcoming infidelity and trust issues requires a commitment to personal growth and relationship building. By working together with your partner and seeking support from mental health professionals, men can learn to trust again and build stronger, healthier relationships.

Stress and Burnout Prevention

Stress and burnout can have a significant impact on men's mental health. Stress can arise from various sources, including work, family, finances, and other life events. Burnout, on the other hand, is a state of emotional, physical, and mental exhaustion caused by prolonged stress. It can affect a person's ability to function and lead to a range of mental health problems, including depression, anxiety, and addiction.

Preventing stress and burnout requires a holistic approach that includes physical, emotional, and mental self-care. Here are some tips on how to prevent stress and burnout:

1. Get enough sleep: Sleep is crucial for mental and physical well-being. Make sure you get at least 7-8 hours of sleep every night.

2. Exercise regularly: Exercise is a natural stress reliever that can improve your mood and boost your energy levels. Aim for at least 30 minutes of physical activity every day.

3. Eat a healthy diet: Eating a balanced diet that includes fruits, vegetables, whole grains, and lean protein can help reduce stress and improve your overall health.

4. Take breaks: Taking regular breaks throughout the day can help reduce stress and prevent burnout. Take a walk, meditate, or do something that relaxes you.

5. Practice mindfulness: Mindfulness is the practice of being present in the moment and paying attention to your thoughts and feelings. It can help reduce stress and improve mental clarity.

6. Set boundaries: Setting boundaries around your work and personal life can help prevent burnout. Learn to say no to things that don't align with your priorities.

7. Seek support: Don't be afraid to reach out for support when you're feeling stressed or overwhelmed. Talk to a friend, family member, or mental health professional.

By taking care of yourself and practicing self-care, you can prevent stress and burnout and improve your mental health. Remember that it's okay to prioritize your well-being and take breaks when you need them. Your mental health is just as important as your physical health.

Identifying sources of stress

Identifying sources of stress is crucial when it comes to managing and preventing mental health issues in men. Stress can be caused by a variety of factors, including work- related issues, relationship problems, financial difficulties, and health concerns.

Identifying the sources of stress is the first step in addressing them and finding solutions.

In the workplace, stress can be caused by a demanding workload, long hours, difficult coworkers, or a toxic work environment. It is important to communicate with your employer and colleagues about what you need to feel supported and productive. Taking breaks, prioritizing tasks, and delegating responsibilities can also be helpful strategies.

Relationship problems, whether with a partner, family member, or friend, can be a major source of stress. Communication is key in addressing these issues. It is important to express your needs and concerns and to actively listen to the other person's perspective. Seeking the help of a therapist or counselor can also be beneficial in resolving conflicts and improving communication.

Financial difficulties, such as debt or unemployment, can also cause stress. Developing a budget and seeking financial counseling can help alleviate some of this stress and provide a sense of control over the situation.

Health concerns, whether physical or mental, can also be a significant source of stress. It is important to prioritize self-care and seek medical attention when necessary. Engaging in regular exercise, eating a healthy diet, and getting enough sleep can also help manage stress and improve overall well-being.

Identifying sources of stress is not always easy, but it is an important step in managing and preventing mental health issues in men. Seeking support from loved ones, mental health professionals, or support groups can also be beneficial in coping with stress and improving mental health.

Coping strategies and self-care practices

Coping strategies and self-care practices are essential for men's mental health and wellbeing. Men often face unique challenges and stressors that can impact their mental health and lead to conditions such as depression, anxiety, PTSD, and substance abuse.

However, by implementing effective coping strategies and self-care practices, men can improve their mental health and lead a happier, healthier life.

One effective coping strategy for men is to develop a support system. Men often feel pressure to be strong and self-reliant, but it's important to remember that seeking support is not a sign of weakness. Whether it's through therapy, support groups, or confiding in trusted friends and family members, having a support system can provide a safe space for men to share their thoughts and feelings and receive guidance and encouragement.

Another essential self-care practice for men is physical activity. Exercise has been shown to have numerous mental health benefits, including reducing symptoms of depression and anxiety, improving mood, and boosting self-esteem. Whether it's hitting the gym, going for a run, or playing a sport, regular physical activity can be an effective way to manage stress and improve overall mental health.

Mindfulness and meditation practices can also be beneficial for men's mental health. These practices can help men develop greater self-awareness, reduce stress, and improve focus and concentration. Mindfulness practices can be as simple as taking a few deep breaths or practicing gratitude each day, while meditation can involve more structured practices such as guided meditations or attending a meditation class.

Finally, it's important for men to prioritize self-care and relaxation. This can involve engaging in activities such as reading, taking a bath, or spending time in nature. By taking time to relax and recharge, men can reduce stress and improve their overall mental health and wellbeing.

In conclusion, coping strategies and self-care practices are essential for men's mental health. By developing a support system, engaging in physical activity, practicing mindfulness and meditation, and prioritizing self-care and relaxation, men can improve their mental health and lead a happier, healthier life. It's important for men to prioritize their mental health and seek support when needed, as mental health is just as important as physical health.

Suicide Prevention and Crisis Intervention

Suicide is a serious issue that affects many people, including men. According to the American Foundation for Suicide Prevention, men die by suicide 3.5 times more often than women. It's important for men's mental health to know how to prevent suicide and intervene in a crisis.

One way to prevent suicide is to recognize the warning signs. Some of the warning signs include talking about wanting to die or feeling hopeless, withdrawing from friends and family, giving away possessions, and engaging in risky behavior. If you notice these warning signs in yourself or someone else, it's important to seek help immediately.

Crisis intervention is also crucial in preventing suicide. If you or someone you know is in crisis, there are several resources available. The National Suicide Prevention Lifeline is a 24/7 hotline that provides free and confidential support for people in distress. The Crisis Text Line also provides free and confidential support via text message.

In addition to seeking help during a crisis, it's also important to take steps to prevent future crises. This may include seeking therapy, building a support network, and developing coping skills. Men's mental health can benefit from talking to a therapist or counselor who can help them work through their emotions and develop healthy coping strategies.

It's also important to prioritize self-care and reduce stress. This may involve practicing mindfulness, getting regular exercise, and taking time for hobbies and relaxation. Men's mental health can benefit from learning to manage their stress and prioritize their mental well-being.

In conclusion, suicide prevention and crisis intervention are crucial for men's mental health. Recognizing warning signs, seeking help during a crisis, and taking steps to prevent future crises can all make a difference. Men's mental health can benefit from prioritizing self-care, seeking therapy, and building a support network. With the right resources and support, suicide can be prevented and men can lead happy and fulfilling lives.

Warning Signs and Risk Factors

Mental health disorders are complex and multifactorial. There is no single cause for any mental health condition, but rather a combination of genetic, environmental, and psychological factors. Nevertheless, there are some warning signs and risk factors that men should be aware of to prevent the onset or exacerbation of mental health problems.

Depression and Anxiety in Men

Depression and anxiety are two of the most common mental health conditions affecting men. The symptoms of depression in men may include feelings of sadness, hopelessness, guilt, or worthlessness, changes in appetite and sleep patterns, loss of interest in activities, fatigue, and suicidal ideation. Anxiety, on the other hand, may manifest as excessive worry, fear, or panic, physical symptoms such as sweating, shaking, or palpitations, and avoidance of certain situations.

Men's PTSD and Trauma

Post-traumatic stress disorder (PTSD) is a mental health condition that can develop after a person has experienced or witnessed a traumatic event. Men who have served in the military, law enforcement, or emergency services are at a higher risk of developing PTSD than the general population. Symptoms of PTSD may include flashbacks, nightmares, hypervigilance, emotional numbness, and avoidance of triggers.

Men's Anger Management and Emotional Regulation

Anger is a normal human emotion that can become problematic when it is expressed in unhealthy ways. Men who struggle with anger management may have difficulty regulating their emotions, and may resort to verbal or physical aggression, substance abuse, or self-harm. Learning healthy coping strategies and communication skills can help men manage their anger and improve their relationships.

Men's Addiction and Substance Abuse

Substance abuse is a common problem among men, and may be a way of coping with underlying mental health issues such as depression, anxiety, or trauma. Men who struggle with addiction may experience withdrawal symptoms, cravings, and social, financial, or legal consequences.

Men's Relationship and Marriage Counseling

Relationships are a crucial aspect of men's mental health, and can have a significant impact on their well-being. Men who struggle with communication, intimacy, or conflict resolution in their relationships may benefit from counseling or therapy. Marriage counseling can also help couples improve their communication, strengthen their bond, and navigate challenges such as infidelity, trust issues, or parenting.

Men's Stress and Burnout Prevention

Stress is a common experience for men in today's fast-paced and demanding society. Prolonged or chronic stress can lead to burnout, a state of physical, emotional, and mental exhaustion. Men who experience stress or burnout may benefit from stress reduction techniques such as mindfulness, exercise, relaxation, or time management.

Men's Suicide Prevention and Crisis Intervention

Suicide is a serious and preventable public health issue affecting men of all ages. Men are more likely than women to die by suicide, and may exhibit warning signs such as depression, anxiety, substance abuse, social isolation, or giving away possessions. Crisis intervention services such as hotlines, counseling, or emergency services can provide immediate support and resources for men in crisis.

Men's Body Image and Self-Esteem

Body image and self-esteem are important aspects of men's mental health, and can be negatively impacted by societal pressures and expectations. Men who struggle with body dissatisfaction, eating disorders, or low self-esteem may benefit from therapy or support groups that promote self-acceptance, positive body image, and self-care.

Men's Career and Workplace Mental Health

Work and career are important sources of identity, purpose, and fulfillment for many men. However, workplace stress, discrimination, or burnout can have a negative impact on their mental health. Employers can promote men's mental health by providing supportive work environments, flexible schedules, mental health resources, and employee assistance programs.

Men's Spirituality and Mindfulness Practices

Spirituality and mindfulness practices such as meditation, yoga, or prayer can promote men's mental health by reducing stress, enhancing self-awareness, and fostering a sense of connection and meaning. Men who are interested in spirituality or mindfulness can explore different practices and traditions that resonate with their beliefs and values.

How to Help Someone in Crisis

We all have faced crisis at some point in our lives, whether it's the loss of a loved one, a job, or a relationship. For men, dealing with crisis can be especially difficult due to societal expectations that men should be strong and not show vulnerability. However, it's important to remember that seeking help during a crisis is a sign of strength and not weakness.

If you know someone who is going through a crisis, here are some ways to help:

1. Listen and be supportive: The most important thing you can do is to listen to the person without judgment. Let them know that you are there for them and that you care.

2. Encourage them to seek professional help: While you can provide emotional support, a mental health professional is trained to provide the necessary support and resources to help someone in crisis.

3. Offer practical help: Offer to help them with practical tasks such as cooking, cleaning, or running errands. This can help alleviate some of the stress they may be feeling.

4. Be patient: Recovery from a crisis takes time, and it's important to be patient and understanding. Don't push someone to "get over it" or "move on" before they are ready.

5. Take care of yourself: Helping someone in crisis can be emotionally taxing. It's important to take care of yourself and seek support if needed.

Remember, helping someone in crisis can make a significant difference in their life. By providing support and resources, you can help them move towards healing and recovery.

Body Image and Self-Esteem

Body image and self-esteem are two concepts that are closely related to men's mental health. Men are often expected to adhere to certain physical standards that can lead to body dissatisfaction and low self-esteem. This can be especially true for men who suffer from mental health disorders such as depression, anxiety, PTSD, and addiction.

Body image refers to how a person perceives their physical appearance, while self- esteem refers to how a person values themselves as a whole. These two concepts can be influenced by a range of factors, including social media, cultural expectations, and personal experiences.

For men who struggle with body image and self-esteem, the negative impact can be significant. Low self-esteem can lead to feelings of worthlessness and a lack of confidence, which can make it difficult to take on new challenges or pursue personal goals. It can also lead to self-destructive behaviors such as substance abuse, disordered eating, and risky sexual behavior.

One of the biggest challenges facing men who struggle with body image and self- esteem is the stigma surrounding mental health. Many men feel ashamed or embarrassed to seek help for their mental health issues, which can make it difficult to access the resources they need to improve their mental health.

However, there are many strategies that men can use to improve their body image and self-esteem. These include practicing self-care, engaging in physical activity, seeking professional help, and challenging negative self-talk.

It's important for men to remember that they are not alone in their struggles with body image and self-esteem. By reaching out for help and support, they can take the first step towards improving their mental health and living a happier, more fulfilling life.

In conclusion, body image and self-esteem are crucial components of men's mental health. By addressing these issues and seeking support when needed, men can take control of their mental health and improve their overall well-being.

Cultural and societal influences on body image

Cultural and societal influences on body image have a significant impact on men's mental health. The perception of the ideal male body has changed over the years, and it has led to a rise in body dissatisfaction and body shaming amongst men. Cultural and societal pressures dictate that men should be muscular, lean, and have a chiseled physique. This is an unrealistic and unattainable standard for most men, and it has led to an increase in eating disorders, anxiety, and depression.

Men are constantly bombarded with images of the "perfect" male body through social media, advertising, and entertainment. These images create an impossible standard that causes men to feel inadequate or less masculine. This can lead to negative body image, low self-esteem, and poor mental health.

Societal expectations also play a role in men's body image. Men are often expected to be tough and emotionless, which can make it difficult for them to express their insecurities about their bodies. This can lead to a sense of shame and embarrassment, which can further damage their mental health.

Moreover, cultural and societal influences on body image can also impact men's relationships and career prospects. Men who do not fit the ideal male body type may feel less attractive or less confident, which can impact their ability to form healthy relationships or succeed in the workplace.

It is essential to recognize the cultural and societal influences on body image and to challenge these unrealistic and harmful standards. Men should be encouraged to accept their bodies and embrace their individuality. They should be provided with resources and support to improve their mental health and body image, such as therapy, counseling, and mindfulness practices.

Breaking the stigma around men's mental health is crucial to creating a society that values and supports men's emotional well-being. By challenging cultural and societal influences on body image, we can create a healthier and more accepting environment for men to thrive in.

Building self-esteem and self-acceptance

Building self-esteem and self-acceptance is a crucial aspect of men's mental health. It is common for men to struggle with confidence and self-worth due to societal expectations and gender norms. However, it is important to understand that self-esteem is not something that can be given to you by others, but rather something that you have to cultivate within yourself.

One way to improve self-esteem is to focus on your strengths and accomplishments rather than your weaknesses and failures. Make a list of your achievements, no matter how small they may seem, and remind yourself of them when you are feeling down.

Additionally, it is important to practice self-compassion and treat yourself with kindness and understanding.

Self-acceptance is another important aspect of building self-esteem. Accepting yourself for who you are, flaws and all, can be difficult but it is essential for mental well-being. It is important to recognize that everyone has imperfections and that they do not define your worth as a person.

Mindfulness practices can also be beneficial for building self-esteem and self-acceptance. Mindfulness involves being present in the moment and accepting your thoughts and feelings without judgment. This can help you become more aware of your negative self- talk and replace it with positive affirmations.

In addition to these practices, seeking therapy or counseling can also be helpful in building self-esteem and self-acceptance. A mental health professional can provide guidance and support in developing a positive self-image and improving your mental well-being.

Overall, building self-esteem and self-acceptance is a journey that requires effort and dedication. However, the benefits of a positive self-image are invaluable and can lead to improved mental health and a happier life.

Addressing eating disorders and body dysmorphia

Eating disorders and body dysmorphia are often thought of as issues that only affect women, but men are just as susceptible to these conditions. In fact, studies show that up to 25% of individuals with an eating disorder are male. Eating disorders and body dysmorphia are serious mental health conditions that can have a significant impact on a person's physical and emotional wellbeing. In this subchapter, we will explore these conditions and provide tips on how to address them.

Eating disorders

Eating disorders are mental health conditions that are characterized by an unhealthy relationship with food. They can take many forms, including anorexia nervosa, bulimia nervosa, and binge eating disorder. These conditions can have serious physical and mental health consequences and can even be life-threatening.

Eating disorders often develop as a way to cope with other mental health issues, such as anxiety, depression, or trauma. They can also be triggered by societal pressure to conform to a certain body type. Men who feel pressure to have a muscular physique may be particularly vulnerable to developing an eating disorder.

If you or someone you know is struggling with an eating disorder, it is important to seek professional help. Treatment typically involves a combination of therapy, medication, and support from loved ones. It is also important to address any underlying mental health issues that may be contributing to the eating disorder.

Body dysmorphia

Body dysmorphia is a condition in which a person becomes obsessed with perceived flaws in their appearance. They may spend hours each day checking and re-checking their appearance in the mirror, seeking validation from others, and engaging in behaviors such as excessive exercise or cosmetic procedures to try to fix their perceived flaws.

Body dysmorphia can have a significant impact on a person's mental health, causing them to feel anxious, depressed, and socially isolated. Men who feel pressure to conform to a certain body type, such as having a muscular physique, may be particularly vulnerable to developing body dysmorphia.

If you or someone you know is struggling with body dysmorphia, it is important to seek professional help. Treatment typically involves therapy, medication, and support from loved ones. It is also important to address any underlying mental health issues that may be contributing to the body dysmorphia.

Conclusion

Eating disorders and body dysmorphia are serious mental health conditions that can have a significant impact on a person's physical and emotional wellbeing. If you or someone you know is struggling with these conditions, it is important to seek professional help. Treatment typically involves a combination of therapy, medication, and support from loved ones. It is also important to address any underlying mental health issues that may be contributing to these conditions. With the right support and treatment, it is possible to overcome eating disorders and body dysmorphia and live a healthy, fulfilling life.

Men's Mental Health in the Workplace

The Impact of Work on Men's Mental Health

In today's fast-paced and competitive world, work plays a significant role in a man's life. For many men, work is not just a source of income but also a source of identity and purpose. However, the pressures and demands of work can also have a significant impact on a man's mental health.

Depression and Anxiety in Men

The pressure to perform and meet deadlines can cause stress and anxiety in men. The fear of failure and the need to meet expectations can lead to depression and anxiety. Men may feel overwhelmed and powerless, resulting in feelings of helplessness, hopelessness, and worthlessness.

Men's PTSD and Trauma

Traumatic events at work, such as workplace accidents or witnessing violence, can cause PTSD in men. The symptoms of PTSD can include flashbacks, nightmares, and feelings of guilt and shame. Men may also experience emotional numbness and detachment, making it difficult to connect with others.

Men's Anger Management and Emotional Regulation

Work can be a source of frustration and anger. Men may feel angry when dealing with difficult clients or coworkers, underperforming colleagues, or unrealistic expectations. Men who struggle with anger management may lash out, causing conflict and damaging relationships.

Men's Addiction and Substance Abuse

The pressures of work can also lead to substance abuse, such as alcohol and drugs. Men may turn to substances to cope with stress, anxiety, and depression. However, addiction can make problems worse, leading to more significant mental health issues.

Men's Relationship and Marriage Counseling

The stress of work can spill over into a man's personal life, causing conflict and strain in relationships. Men may struggle to balance work and family responsibilities, leading to feelings of guilt and frustration. Relationship and marriage counseling can help men improve communication, manage stress, and strengthen relationships.

Men's Stress and Burnout Prevention

Stress and burnout can have a significant impact on a man's mental health. Men who experience burnout may feel emotionally drained, cynical, and detached from work.

Prevention measures such as self-care, time management, and relaxation techniques can help men manage stress and prevent burnout.

Men's Suicide Prevention and Crisis Intervention

Work-related stress and mental health issues can lead to thoughts of suicide. Men may feel overwhelmed and hopeless, leading to suicidal ideation. Suicide prevention and crisis intervention programs can help men get the support they need during a mental health crisis.

Men's Body Image and Self-Esteem

The pressure to look and perform a certain way at work can impact a man's body image and self-esteem. Men may feel pressure to have a certain body type or maintain a specific image, leading to feelings of inadequacy and low self-esteem.

Men's Career and Workplace Mental Health

Employers have a responsibility to support the mental health of their employees. Creating a positive workplace culture that prioritizes mental health can improve employee well-being and productivity.

Men's Spirituality and Mindfulness Practices

Spirituality and mindfulness practices can help men manage stress and improve mental health. Activities such as meditation, yoga, and journaling can help men connect with their emotions and improve overall well-being.

In conclusion, work can have a significant impact on a man's mental health. Men must prioritize their mental health and seek help when needed. Employers must also prioritize the mental health of their employees, creating a positive workplace culture that supports employee well-being.

Creating a Supportive Work Environment

A supportive work environment can have a significant impact on men's mental health. When employees feel supported and valued, they are more likely to experience less stress, anxiety, and depression in the workplace. Creating a supportive work environment requires a collaborative effort from employers and employees. Here are some tips on how to create a supportive work environment:

1. Encourage Open Communication

Encourage open communication between employees and management. This can be done by creating an open-door policy where employees can discuss their concerns and ideas with management. By doing so, employees feel heard and valued, which can promote a positive work environment.

2. Provide Mental Health Resources

Provide mental health resources such as an employee assistance program (EAP) or access to mental health professionals. This can help employees who are struggling with mental health issues get the support they need.

3. Offer Flexible Work Arrangements

Offering flexible work arrangements such as remote work or flexible schedules can help employees manage their work-life balance. This can reduce stress and promote better mental health.

4. Encourage Social Connections

Encourage social connections between employees by organizing team-building activities or social events. This can help build a positive work culture and foster a sense of community.

5. Address Workplace Stressors

Address workplace stressors such as workload, unrealistic deadlines, or inadequate training. By addressing these stressors, employees are less likely to experience burnout and other mental health issues.

Creating a supportive work environment is crucial for men's mental health. By encouraging open communication, providing mental health resources, offering flexible work arrangements, encouraging social connections, and addressing workplace stressors, employers can help create a positive work environment that promotes mental well- being.

Strategies for managing work-related stress and burnout

Work-related stress and burnout can be detrimental to men's mental health, affecting not only their job performance but also their personal relationships and overall quality of life. It is crucial for men to understand the strategies for managing work-related stress and burnout to maintain their mental health and wellbeing.

1. Set boundaries

Setting boundaries is critical to managing work-related stress and burnout. It is vital to create a work-life balance by setting aside time for personal activities, hobbies, and relaxation. It is also essential to learn to say "no" to additional work responsibilities that may be beyond one's capacity.

2. Practice self-care

Self-care is an essential aspect of managing work-related stress and burnout. It is crucial to prioritize self-care activities such as exercise, proper nutrition, and adequate sleep.

Engaging in activities that bring joy and relaxation such as reading, listening to music, or taking a warm bath can also help reduce stress.

3. Seek support

Seeking support from family, friends, or a mental health professional can be beneficial in managing work-related stress and burnout. It is essential to communicate feelings and concerns to someone who can provide emotional support and practical solutions.

4. Mindfulness and meditation

Mindfulness and meditation practices have been shown to reduce stress and improve mental health. Practicing mindfulness through activities such as yoga, meditation, or deep breathing exercises can help reduce stress and increase resilience.

5. Prioritize time management

Effective time management is crucial in managing work-related stress and burnout. It is essential to prioritize tasks, delegate responsibilities, and avoid procrastination to reduce stress and increase productivity.

6. Take breaks

Taking breaks throughout the workday is essential for reducing stress and increasing productivity. Taking a short walk, stretching, or engaging in a brief relaxation exercise can help reduce stress and improve mental clarity.

In conclusion, managing work-related stress and burnout is essential for men's mental health and wellbeing. By setting boundaries, practicing self-care, seeking support, engaging in mindfulness and meditation practices, prioritizing time management, and taking breaks, men can reduce stress and achieve a healthy work-life balance.

Spirituality and Mindfulness Practices

The Role of Spirituality in Men's Mental Health

Spirituality can be defined as the search for meaning and purpose in life, and the belief in something greater than oneself. It can take many forms, such as religion, meditation, or nature, and can be a powerful tool for men's mental health.

In today's fast-paced and stressful world, many men struggle with mental health issues such as depression, anxiety, PTSD, anger management, addiction, and burnout. While traditional forms of therapy and medication can be helpful, spirituality can provide a unique and complementary approach to healing.

One way spirituality can benefit men's mental health is by providing a sense of connection and community. For example, participating in a religious or spiritual group can provide a sense of belonging and support, which can help men feel less alone in their struggles. Additionally, spiritual practices such as meditation and mindfulness can help men cultivate a deeper sense of self-awareness and emotional regulation, which can improve their overall mental health.

Spirituality can also provide men with a sense of purpose and meaning in life. When men feel like their lives have a greater purpose, they may be more motivated to overcome challenges and persevere through difficult times. Additionally, spiritual practices can help men develop a sense of gratitude and appreciation for the present moment, which can help combat feelings of stress and burnout.

For men who have experienced trauma or are struggling with addiction, spirituality can be a powerful tool for healing and recovery. Many men find that participating in spiritual practices such as prayer, meditation, or nature walks can help them find peace and healing in the aftermath of trauma or addiction.

In conclusion, spirituality can play an important role in men's mental health. By providing a sense of connection, purpose, and healing, spiritual practices can complement traditional forms of therapy and medication and provide men with a holistic approach to mental health and wellness.

Mindfulness practices for stress reduction and emotional regulation

Mindfulness practices are becoming increasingly popular in the world of mental health and are highly effective in reducing stress and regulating emotions. Mindfulness is a practice that involves focusing on the present moment, without judgment or distraction. It is a way to observe and accept our thoughts, emotions, and physical sensations without reacting to them.

For men struggling with mental health issues such as depression, anxiety, PTSD, anger management, addiction, and burnout, mindfulness can be an effective tool to help manage symptoms and improve overall well-being. Here are some mindfulness practices that men can try:

1. Mindful breathing: Take a few minutes each day to focus on your breath. Notice the sensation of the air moving in and out of your body. If your mind wanders, gently bring it back to your breath.

2. Body scan: Lie down or sit comfortably and focus on different parts of your body, starting from your toes and moving up to your head. Notice any sensations or areas of tension and try to release them.

3. Gratitude practice: Take a few minutes each day to reflect on things you are grateful for. This can be anything from a supportive friend to a beautiful sunset.

4. Mindful movement: Engage in physical activities such as yoga, tai chi, or walking meditation. Focus on the sensation of your body moving and the rhythm of your breath.

Mindful eating: Pay attention to the taste, smell, and texture of your food. Take time to savor each bite and notice how it makes you feel.

In addition to these practices, men can also benefit from incorporating mindfulness into their daily routines. This can include taking a few minutes each day to practice gratitude, setting intentions for the day, and taking breaks throughout the day to check in with themselves.

It is important to note that mindfulness is not a cure-all for mental health issues and should not be used as a replacement for professional treatment. However, it can be a helpful tool to supplement therapy and medication.

Overall, mindfulness can be a powerful tool for men to manage stress, regulate emotions, and improve overall well-being. By incorporating mindfulness practices into their daily routines, men can take control of their mental health and break the stigma surrounding men's mental health issues.

Incorporating spirituality and mindfulness into daily life

Incorporating spirituality and mindfulness into daily life can be a powerful tool for improving men's mental health. This approach involves a shift in perspective — from the external world to the internal world.

Spirituality can be defined as a connection to something greater than oneself, whether it be a higher power, nature, or the universe. Mindfulness, on the other hand, is the practice of being present in the moment and observing one's thoughts and emotions without judgment.

Both spirituality and mindfulness can help men develop a deeper sense of self- awareness, which is essential for managing mental health issues such as depression, anxiety, PTSD, and addiction.

One way to incorporate spirituality into daily life is through meditation or prayer. Taking a few minutes each day to quiet the mind and connect with a higher power can help men feel more grounded and centered.

Mindfulness can be practiced in a variety of ways, such as through mindful breathing or mindful eating. By paying attention to the present moment, men can learn to recognize and manage their thoughts and emotions more effectively.

Incorporating spirituality and mindfulness into daily life can also be helpful for men struggling with anger management and emotional regulation. By learning to observe their thoughts and emotions without judgment, men can develop greater self-control and reduce the likelihood of reacting impulsively.

Relationship and marriage counseling can also benefit from incorporating spirituality and mindfulness practices. By developing a deeper sense of self-awareness, men can better understand their own needs and communicate them effectively to their partners.

Stress and burnout prevention can also be improved through spirituality and mindfulness practices. By learning to manage stress in a healthy way, such as through meditation or yoga, men can prevent burnout and maintain a healthy work-life balance.

Finally, spirituality and mindfulness can be powerful tools for men struggling with body image and self-esteem issues. By developing a deeper connection to their inner selves, men can learn to value themselves for who they are rather than how they look.

In conclusion, incorporating spirituality and mindfulness into daily life can be a powerful tool for improving men's mental health. By developing greater self-awareness, managing stress and emotions effectively, and connecting with something greater than themselves, men can better manage a variety of mental health issues and lead happier, healthier lives.

Conclusion

The importance of breaking the stigma surrounding men's mental health

The importance of breaking the stigma surrounding men's mental health cannot be overstated. For far too long, men have been conditioned to believe that expressing emotions is a weakness, and seeking help for mental health issues is a sign of failure. This kind of toxic masculinity has created a culture of silence around men's mental health, which has led to devastating consequences.

Men's mental health is a complex issue that affects millions of men worldwide. Depression and anxiety in men are common, but many men feel ashamed to seek help or talk about their struggles. Men's PTSD and trauma are also prevalent, particularly among those who have served in the armed forces or experienced violence or abuse.

Men's anger management and emotional regulation are also important topics, as men are often taught to suppress their emotions rather than learn how to manage them in a healthy way.

Men's addiction and substance abuse are also significant concerns, as men are more likely than women to struggle with addiction. Men's relationship and marriage counseling is another area where mental health can have a significant impact, as poor mental health can contribute to relationship problems. Men's stress and burnout prevention are also critical, as men often feel pressure to be the primary breadwinners and may struggle to balance work and personal life.

Perhaps the most alarming consequence of the stigma surrounding men's mental health is the high rate of suicide among men. Men are more likely to die by suicide than women, and this is often due to the fact that they feel unable to seek help or talk about their struggles.

Breaking the stigma surrounding men's mental health is essential for improving the lives of millions of men worldwide. By encouraging men to talk about their mental health struggles and seeking help when needed, we can reduce the negative impact of toxic masculinity and improve men's overall well-being. We must also work to create more inclusive mental health services that are tailored to men's unique needs and experiences. By doing so, we can create a world where men feel empowered to take care of their mental health and live happy, fulfilling lives.

Encouraging Men to Seek Help and Support

It is often said that men are expected to be strong and stoic, and that seeking help or support is considered a sign of weakness. This stigma around mental health can be especially harmful to men, who may feel isolated and unable to seek the help they need when struggling with depression, anxiety, PTSD, anger management, addiction, relationship issues, burnout, or suicidal thoughts. However, it is important to understand that seeking help is a sign of strength, and that there are many resources available for men who need support.

One way to encourage men to seek help is to educate them about the benefits of therapy, counseling, and other forms of mental health treatment. These treatments can provide a safe space for men to express their feelings and work through their issues, and can help them develop coping strategies and improve their overall wellbeing. Men should also be encouraged to seek support from friends, family members, and support groups, as these can provide a sense of community and belonging that can be invaluable in times of need.

Another way to encourage men to seek help is to reduce the stigma around mental health by promoting open and honest conversations about mental health and wellbeing. Men should feel comfortable sharing their struggles and seeking help without fear of judgment or shame. This can be achieved by normalizing discussions about mental health in the media, in the workplace, and in social settings, and by providing accurate information about mental health and the resources available for those who need them.

Finally, men should be encouraged to prioritize self-care and self-compassion, and to recognize the importance of taking care of their mental health. This can include engaging in mindfulness practices, seeking out hobbies and activities that bring joy and fulfillment, and setting boundaries and limits to prevent burnout and stress. By promoting a culture of self-care and self-compassion, men can learn to prioritize their mental health and wellbeing, and to seek help and support when they need it.

In conclusion, it is important to encourage men to seek help and support for their mental health, and to reduce the stigma around mental health that can prevent men from seeking the help they need. By promoting open and honest conversations about mental health, providing accurate information about mental health resources, and encouraging self-care and self-compassion, we can help men to prioritize their mental health and wellbeing, and to live happier, healthier lives.

Resources for men's mental health support and treatment

It is important to recognize that seeking help for mental health concerns is a sign of strength, not weakness. However, many men may feel hesitant or embarrassed to reach out for support. Fortunately, there are numerous resources available to help men prioritize their mental health and wellbeing.

Therapy and Counseling

One of the most effective forms of mental health support and treatment is therapy or counseling. Men can benefit from talking to a licensed therapist or counselor who can help them explore and process their emotions, develop coping skills, and work towards their goals. There are many different types of therapy available, including cognitive- behavioral therapy (CBT), which focuses on changing negative thought patterns, and mindfulness-based therapies, which help individuals develop present-moment awareness and acceptance.

Online Resources

For men who may not feel comfortable attending therapy in person, there are many online resources available. These include apps and websites that offer guided meditations, stress management techniques, and self-help resources. Some popular options include Headspace, Calm, and Talkspace.

Support Groups

Men can also benefit from connecting with others who are going through similar experiences. Support groups provide a safe and non-judgmental space for individuals to share their feelings and receive support from others. There are support groups available for a wide range of mental health concerns, including depression, anxiety, PTSD, addiction, and more.

Community Resources

Local community resources can also be a valuable source of support for men struggling with mental health concerns. This may include community mental health centers, crisis hotlines, and other non-profit organizations that offer mental health services. Many workplaces and schools also offer Employee Assistance Programs (EAPs) that provide confidential counseling services to employees and their families.

In conclusion, there are many resources available to help men prioritize their mental health and wellbeing. Whether seeking therapy, utilizing online resources, joining a support group, or accessing community resources, men should feel empowered to seek the help and support they need to live a happy and healthy life.